2.1

2mig 74446

D1035633

4446

00-201
599.5   Ruffin, Frances E.
R
Whales = Ballenas

Bilingual Edition

My World of
ANIMALS™

Edición Bilingüe

WHALES
BALLENAS

FRANCES E. RUFFIN
TRADUCCIÓN AL ESPAÑOL:
NATHALIE BEULLENS

The Rosen Publishing Group's
PowerKids Press™ & **Editorial Buenas Letras**™
New York

For Davey Woods

Published in 2004 by The Rosen Publishing Group, Inc.
29 East 21st Street, New York, NY 10010

First Edition

Book Design: Mike Donnellan
Illustration by Mike Donnellan

Photo Credits:Cover, p. 17 © Hiroya Minakuchi/Seapics.com/Innerspace Visions; p. 5 © Mike Johnson/Innerspace Visions; p. 12 © Philip Colla/Innerspace Visions; p. 9 © Amos Nachoum/CORBIS; p. 11 © Kenna Ward/CORBIS; p. 13 © Tom Brakefield/CORBIS; p. 15 © Ron Sanford/CORBIS; p. 19 © Sea World of California/CORBIS; p. 21 © Paul A. Souders/CORBIS.

Ruffin, Frances E.
Whales = Ballenas / Frances E. Ruffin ; translated by Nathalie Beullens.
p. cm. — (My world of animals)
Includes bibliographical references and index.
Summary: This book introduces whales, describing their behavior and their songs.
ISBN 1-4042-7520-7 (lib.)
1. Whales—Juvenile literature   [1. Whales 2. Spanish language materials—Bilingual]
I. Title II. Title: Ballenas   III. Series
QL737.C4 R85 2004   2003-010271
599.5—dc21

Manufactured in the United States of America

CONTENTS

CONTENIDO

The blue whale is the largest animal on Earth. A blue whale can be 100 feet (30 m) long. That's longer than two school buses.

La ballena azul es el animal más grande de la Tierra. Una ballena azul puede llegar a medir hasta 100 pies (30 m) de largo. Más que dos autobuses de escuela.

Whales live in the ocean all of their lives, but they are not fish. They are animals called mammals. People are mammals, too.

Las ballenas viven toda su vida en el océano, pero no son peces. Son animales llamados mamíferos. Los humanos también somos mamíferos.

7

Whales breathe air. They feed their babies milk. All mammals do these things.

Las ballenas respiran aire. Además le dan leche a sus bebés, como todos los mamíferos.

A whale breathes through one or two blowholes in its head. Whales also blow clouds of water into the air.

Las ballenas respiran a través de uno o dos orificios que tienen en la cabeza. Las ballenas soplan vapor de agua que sale en forma de chorro.

11

Some whales have teeth. They use their teeth to catch and eat fish and small sea animals.

Algunas ballenas tienen dientes. Usan sus dientes para atrapar y comer peces y pequeños animales acuáticos.

13

Other whales use a baleen to eat. This is a bony screen in their mouths. It lets water run out, but holds in tiny sea plants and animals.

Otras ballenas utilizan unas barbas para comer. Estas barbas son como un filtro en la boca que deja salir el agua pero atrapa a las plantas y a los pequeños animales acuáticos.

14

15

A sperm whale can dive deeper than 1 mile (1.6 km) to catch food. It can hold its breath for 2 hours at a time!

Los cachalotes pueden sumergirse más de 1 milla (1.6 km) de profundidad para atrapar su comida. ¡Pueden aguantar la respiración hasta por 2 horas!

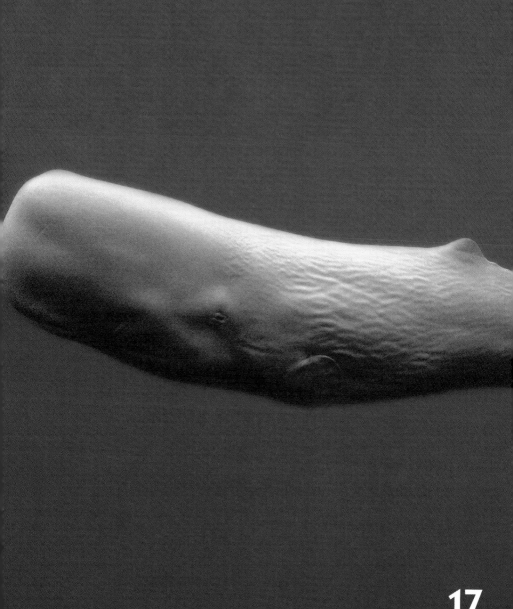

17

Beluga whales are also called white whales. They and other whales make noises that sound like singing. Their songs can be heard from far away.

A las belugas también se les llama ballenas blancas. Estas y otras ballenas hacen sonidos que parecen un canto. Sus canciones se pueden escuchar desde muy lejos.

18

Some whales are put in aquariums where people can see them. People also study whales to learn more about sea animals.

A algunas ballenas se les pone en acuarios para que la gente las pueda ver. La gente también estudia a las ballenas para aprender más sobre los animales acuáticos.

Words to Know
Palabras que debes saber

aquarium
acuario

baleen
barbas

blowholes
orificios

ocean
océano

Here are more books to read about whales/
Otros libros que puedes leer sobre las ballenas:

In English/En inglés:
National Geographic Animal Encyclopedia

Bilingual Books/Libros bilingües:
The Blue Whale / La ballena azul
By Joy Page
PowerKids Press & Editorial Buenas Letras

Due to the changing nature of Internet links, PowerKids Press has developed an online list of Web sites related to the subject of this book. This site is updated regularly. Please use this link to access the list:

http://www.buenasletraslinks.com/mwanim/ballen

Index

Índice

Words in English: 197   Palabras en español: 223

Note to Parents, Teachers, and Librarians

PowerKids Readers books *en español* are specially designed for emergent Hispanic readers and students learning Spanish in the United States. Simple stories and concepts are paired with photographs of real kids in real-life situations. Sentences are short and simple, employing a basic vocabulary of sight words, as well as new words that describe familiar things and places. With their engaging stories and vivid photo-illustrations, PowerKids *en español* gives children the opportunity to develop a love of reading and learning that they will carry with them throughout their lives.